us.

a collection of poetry
by
kiana azizian

for those who couldn't handle my storm,
i'm sorry i was too much for you.

these words,
these pages,
this love,

it was made for
me,
them,
&
you.

they were made for
us.

us.

contents

me.	7
them.	83
you.	185

us.

me.

i'm not really sure
when it all started:
hating myself.
probably somewhere
in between the
you're not pretty enough
and the
eat less.

their words became
too real and began
to consume me.
before i knew it,
they'd taken
over my existence.
they'd defined me.

i shouldn't have
listened to them,
because all their
words were lies.

who were they
to define my
existence?
who were they
to destroy me?

i cannot speak
these words properly.
they never sound
as poetic as i'd like.

so i've written
them out for you.
hear them
how you please.

i have a big heart.
i believe in big love.

- *hopeful romantic*

i'll admit,
i have days where
i loathe myself for
living in extremes,
for caring and
giving too much,
loving too much,
just being too much.

but i'd rather live
in extreme than
locked within
boundaries.
i'd rather feel
too much than
nothing at all.
i'd rather love
too much than
lack affection.
i'd rather be
too much than
not be enough.

these stretch marks
tell my story better
than any words.
the starving
and the binging.
the line between
healthy and skinny.
the battle of
accepting myself-
all of myself.
they will forever
be one with my skin,
beautifully marking
the struggle of learning
to love myself.

i'm not sure
who i am anymore;
maybe i never really was.

but what i do know
is i used to be better
than this.
kinder,
less selfish,
more caring,
warmer.

i think i've gotten
this all backward.
aren't we supposed
to grow with age?
aren't we supposed
to be better as each
year passes?

i can't stay here,
but i'm not sure
where to go.
this body doesn't
seem like
home anymore.

trouble,
i loved the way
he said my name.

it was as if he knew.

i was so young.
i couldn't understand
why these women were
covered from head to toe,
their bodies
hidden from the world,
as if they should be ashamed
of what laid beneath the shawls.

but i'll never forget
the day at the beach,
how fluently they
ripped off their oppression.
sun shining upon
their bare skin,
they'd never
looked so blissful,
so free.

"sin" had never
looked so beautiful.

- *iran*

i don't need a man
to love me right.
i have hands of
my own.

i still remember
the first time they broke me.

i was in seventh grade,
and it was on the bus ride home,
when i found their note.

no one likes you,
their words read,
all signing their names
below like a bloody petition.

i never got the
chance to thank them.

thank you for not being kind.
thank you for showing
me exactly the type of person
i do not want to be.

some days i even scare
myself with these words
and the undeniable
power of my love.
i'll never blame the
ones who left.
for on days like today,
i wish i could run
from my mind,
hide away where
it wouldn't be able
to control me.

his hand felt like a wildfire
burning my bare skin.

you're cold, he stated.

oh yeah,
i forgot my sweater in my car,
i admitted.

no.
you...
you have gone cold.

- wake-up call

my lips never manage
to speak the words my
heart is bleeding to say.

rape does not always
appear as a stranger
in a dark alley;
sometimes he comes
as a familiar face
in a safe place.

the wind is a
mischievous thing.

it feels as if some days
she blows straight through me,
while other days she whispers
all the things i need to hear.

how can i expect you
to love me
when i don't even
love myself?

stop,
i yelled into your face.

you didn't obey.

if anything you went harder,
faster,
harder,
deeper,
harder.

darkness.

this is when I run-
when things have
become too much
and I've destroyed
everything that used
to be whole.

i've messed it all up.
i'll be gone in the morning.
and as you watch
the sunrise alone,
just know my apology
is written within its colors.

they keep telling
me to forget,
to move on.

but how can i let go
when it's his pulse
keeping me alive?

just because we lived
under one roof
doesn't mean our
home wasn't broken.

- *dysfunctional family*

i'm scared by not settling,
i'll never settle down.

keep your thoughts
to yourself,
i've got enough of
my own.

- over-thinker

you're so caught
up in my past,
not able to see
who i presently am.

you didn't even
give me a chance.

- i'm not the person i used to be

i can't help but love
the way the pain
burns my lungs
as i inhale your
secondhand lies.

i'm no longer searching for
monsters under my bed;
i'm looking for demons
between the sheets.

- this bed is no longer safe

when we were
younger we desired
the autonomy of age,
but now we desire
the freedom of
childhood.

- wasted youth

it's on the days my heart
is a bit heavier,
these words become
a bit lighter.

i was raised from a culture
that teaches their women to hide
their bodies and to cover their mouths,
a society teaching young girls
they will never be as superior as men
and suppresses women's rights.

- i am ashamed of my motherland

pretty:
what a little word to describe me.

intelligent,
honest,
loyal,
creative,
eloquent.

i'm so much more than my looks.

my heart pains
for the deserving love
it has yet to receive.

i'm the queen of my own castle.
there's no place for a prince here,
no throne for a king,
just a crown dressed in jewels
and a noble chair fit for me.

i never wanted the fame,
the fortune,
the attention.

i just wanted my
voice to be heard.
i just wanted to
make a difference.

- i just want to change the world

the day you told me this body
was not my own was the day
you taught me it is more my
own than ever before.

talk is cheap.

i'm going broke.

i'm sorry to all the things
i've destroyed trying to
rebuild myself.
i'm sorry to all the ones
i've left trying to
find myself.
i'm sorry to all the hearts
i've broken trying to
understand my own.

they never loved one another.
they did put on a good show for us,
but we secretly always
knew it wasn't the truth.

i'll never be able to repay my mother.

she spent twenty-five years sleeping
next to a man she never loved,
so we could all rest our eyes
under the same roof.

- arranged marriage

i've personally danced
with fate a few too many
times to not believe in the
magic of this world.

she usually preferred
silence to people.
people seemed
to say all the
wrong things;
silence always
 spoke the truth.

this pen has run dry.
these words no longer
make sense.

- writer's block

us.

don't fall for me
because of my body,
or my pretty.
appearances fade.
fall for me:
my brains,
my soul,
my being.
drown in all that makes
me who i am,
not something as
superficial as my looks.

i'm a being of contradictions.
i have an immense heart,
yet block out love.
i care too much,
yet don't give any shits.
i am confident,
yet full of insecurities.
i am strong,
yet have weakness in my bones.
i am happy,
yet dance often with sadness.
i am kind,
yet ruthless.

i can put the world
at your feet,
and i can also pull it
out from under you.

food became the enemy;
calories were everything.

eat less.
get thinner.
try not to take up too much space.
exist small.
be smaller.

- the hungry mind of an eating disorder

she was the crackle of a fire
and the stillness of the ocean.
she could burn down a city,
then drown it with her storms.
she was striking,
like lighting after thunder,
devastation after a hurricane.
the world stopped to watch her live.
it loved the danger in her,
yet was also terrified of her existence.
she was like nothing this earth had ever
experienced before.

and she lived for keeping
the universe on its toes.

some days i don't know
how to exist,
nor do i want to.

- *depression*

you gave me life,
bringing me into this
world on your own.

you are the most
beautiful person
i've ever known.

i love you always.

- to my mother

i'm not a victim,
or a survivor.

i'm not brave,
or strong.

i'm just a little
human,
with a lot more
being.

she let every word
linger on her lips,
as if she always had
something else to say.

the shape and size
of this body will
never convey
its worth.

don't you ever get lonely?
her puddle-filled
eyes asked me.

yes,
i admitted.
but i'd rather drown in
my own loneliness than
by the arms of a man
who can't carry me.

i'm not a tree in a meadow;
i'm the whole damn forest.
i'm the branches
and i'm the leaves,
solid enough to shelter life,
gentle enough to
provide breath.
my feet are rooted in the
depths of the earth.
each year,
i get bigger,
stronger.
i've weathered the
worst of storms,
always holding
my ground.
my heart is made
of kindling spirits.
my love is endlessly
evergreen.

i'm not sure which is worse:
watching the light in my
mother's eyes helplessly fade,
or knowing it was my father
who took it away.

you block out love,
standing behind
locked doors,
wondering why
no one ever gave
you a key.

it's the wild
ones who will
set you free.

she loves
thunderstorms.

they prove even the
heavens lose control
sometimes.

i will wait for you
within the sunflower fields,
where the colors of the
sky caress the sun.
i will wait for you
between the city lights
and the space between
the sea and the horizon.

i will wait for you
in all the places
you've fallen in love.
it is there where i
will be waiting for you.

us.

there's a man who stands
on my neighborhood corner.
every morning,
he waits.
for something,
for someone,
i'm not entirely sure.
but without fail,
he waits.

and i can't help but
think to myself,
how beautiful to love
something so much,
you'd wake up every day,
hoping today,
maybe today,
it would come back to you.

go away.

you're not welcome
here anymore.

- closed-minded

i guess i just woke up one day
and decided i couldn't keep living like this.
i packed my bags
and became one with the road.
they called it running;
i prefer "searching."
i was just looking for more from this life.
i was just looking for me.

truth be told,
i've always felt out of
place in my world.
but out there,
it all made a little more sense.

it was the people and the way they viewed
things the same,
as if i'd finally found my family,
my people.
they opened their arms
and welcomed me home.
they helped heal me.
they created me.
if it wasn't for them, i wouldn't be here.
if it wasn't for the ambiguity of the road,
i'd be more lost than ever.

- *traveling*

she was strong,
yet felt so weak.
every night,
she slept with
tears gushing
from her heart.
but every morning,
she rose with
a smile falling
from her lips.

they threw bricks at me.
i turned them into an empire.

- *look at me now*

i wouldn't take it back,
any of it-
not the struggles
or the tragedies.
this pain is what
got me here.
it shaped me
into who i am.
sorrow taught me
the importance
of happiness;
a desire for
death taught me
the beauty of life;
rock bottom
taught me to enjoy
the view from the top.

if it wasn't for the bad,
i'd never welcome the good.
if it wasn't for the pain,
i'd never believe in the magic.

what's a girl to do
when she has so
much love to offer
and no one to
give it to?

you can't love
me in parts.

take me all,
or walk away
with none.

the more i fall in
love with myself,
the less admiration
i need from others.

she fell in love with a man
who couldn't figure out
how to handle her.
she fell in love with a man
who wasn't strong
enough to carry her.
she fell in love with a man
who wasn't man enough
to love her in return.

i'm stuck between
two worlds:
a desire to go,
the need to stay.

- *this travel bug has infected me*

you're the one
breaking your own heart,
grasping it so close,
never letting anyone else in.
you constantly push them away,
thinking you're protecting yourself
when really you're the reason
its blood has run dry.

us.

i've got a thing for the type of people who are undeniably themselves- the type of people with messy hair and even messier souls, the people who wear their hearts on their chest and passions in their tears. i've got a thing for those people who laugh at their own jokes and rejoice in their own success. the people for me are the ones who fight for what they believe in and never let their spirit settle. i adore all the people who have the strength to remain soft and the fire to burn hard. these are the types of people i'm in love with. these are the types of people i want in my life.

you.

it's always been you.

- a love letter to myself

i want a man who
can carry me,
a man strong enough
to calm my storms,
yet not tame my chaos.
i want a man who
can hear me when
i can't find the words to speak,
and a man who
can love me when
i can't manage to love myself.
i want arms that
feel like home,
and a heart that
beats poetry.
i want eyes that can
carry my tears,
and lips that help me
forget my own name.

i *want* a man like this;
i do not need a man like this.

and this is the most
powerful type of
desire in existence.

i won't keep wasting
my words on people
who don't have the
ears to hear me.

i went to war with the
darkest of my demons.
now i'm left with nothing
but the bones of their skeletons
and echoes of their screams.
i went to war with the little voices
in my head,
the ones convincing me i was
never good enough.
i've been at battle with
myself for years.

i won.
i finally defeated myself.
it was the greatest
victory of my life. she wanted to
change the world.
perhaps,
maybe,
possibly,
these words had the
power to do so.

i'd rather love
myself than
another.

us.

them.

us.

you,
he lied,
are everything
i've ever wanted.

i still remember
the first time i saw you.
your smile was what i fell for.
it used to be my favorite
thing about you.
but now when i look at you,
all i see is heartbreak
and disappointment.
i wish we could go
back to our first day
at our favorite coffee shop,
not so we can undo
this destruction
(we can't change the past),
but just to fall in love
with your smile one last time.

he gave me love.
i gave him the world.

i have a
one-track
mind,
and all
stops lead to
you.

- *all aboard*

all i need is
a little rain,
a little coffee,
and a lot of you.

the room was
our war zone.
the bed was
our battlefield,
fighting,
loving.

we had no
boundaries,
no uncertainties.

we were just
two souls,
combating to
become one.

us.

i told the stars
about you,
and now even
the universe
cannot stop
screaming
your name.

loving you was effortless.

leaving you was heartbreaking.

i'm a sucker for pain,
and you've got blood
painted all over you.

breathe me in.
i want to be your
sole source of life.
take me,
all of me.
mark control
of my existence.
i want to be absorbed
into you,
crawl into your skin
and run through your veins.
i want to be
your better half,
the things you never
knew you needed.
i want to be your last breath
of fresh air,
captivating your lungs.
i want to be the fire
keeping you warm,
the arms holding you close.
take me as yours.
create us
from two into one.

us.

i lost myself
trying to
find
you.

like religion,
i want to
believe
in you,
but don't even
know where
to begin.

you drained me
of all i had.

and now,
i'm not sure what i
have left to give.

when they
ask you
about me,
i hope you
tell them how
i was your
most beautiful
mistake.

- the one that you let get away

us.

why start a battle
if you're not ready
to go to war?

i've seen you before.

maybe in another
life we were lovers.

maybe in that world
we were able to
make us work.

us.

the sun and the moon
had nothing on us.

*what do you think
heaven is like?*
i curiously asked.

*like waking up,
every morning,
next to you,*
he explained.

i gave you a map
of my heart,
which you didn't even
bother to read.
you stomped around
uncharted territories,
planted a white flag,
claimed my land
as your own.

i have to admit,
at the time i liked
how you went places
no one had before.
but you conquered,
then left.
like any other
great explorer,
you made your mark,
leaving this heart more
damaged than ever.

- *mission accomplished*

honestly,
i wasn't ready for you.

but when it is time,
well,
then,
you and i,
we will send this
world up in flames
and set the
universe on fire.

i wake every morning to find
your side of the bed still empty.
it usually takes a few seconds for me to realize
where i am,
where you went.
i take a deep breath and
remind myself it will all be.
it has to all be okay.
then i force myself out of the cold sheets and
make my way to the shower.
i undress myself,
slowly watching my skin revealed naked.
i can't bear to look in the mirror for long.
i don't look like myself anymore.
i haven't for years.
then i step into the shower,
turn the water from cold to hot,
adjusting the temperature
to just the way you used to like it.
then i wash you off my skin,
out of my hair,
and watch as you swirl down the drain.
it has to all be okay.
i can't stay in there for too long because your
memory always comes
and joins me after some time.
so i shut off the water,
shut you off,
and wipe myself dry.
then i force myself to get ready.
it has to all be okay.
the rest of the day feels like a blur.
i know how to act and how to move,
yet i've forgotten how to feel.

they ask me how i am,
and i do the same.
small talk: i've never been a fan.
the day goes on.
and soon enough,
i'm on my way home,
back to the space we used to share,
the place we used to live.
it has to all be okay.
i cook dinner alone,
then eat,
alone.
and once i've cleaned up,
i find myself back in our bed.
my bed.
the tears come without notice,
and i find myself slipping back
into the ocean of grief,
the ocean of you.
it has to all be okay.
i feel like i'm buried alive,
struggling for air,
struggling for life.
but tomorrow is another day,
and every day doesn't hurt as much.
each day,
i forget you a little more.
i feel you a little less.
i love you a little less.

it's all going to be okay.
it has to be.

i gently
planted
our love,
giving it
everything
it ever
needed:
earth,
nurture,
soil,
light.

in the end,
it was you
who didn't
bother to
water it.

your
mind
is still
my
favorite
book
to read.

i rarely allow myself
to go to this place-
the space where our
memories now reside.
so much pain comes
with the beautiful
memory of you.
but on days where
i slip and find myself lost,
those reminders of you
help me find my way
back home.

- repressed memories

your name
is the only word
my mouth knows
how to taste.

i'm starving
for you
on my lips.

us.

you left,
and i'm still alive.

the thing about life
is we always survive.

so much pain
and frustration
fall off the
consonants
of your name.

and on the day
i lost you,
it snowed
for the first
time in years.

even the
universe
felt it too.

i was born with
music blaring
out of me,
but you were too
tone-deaf to hear.

i'm done falling for you.
i'm now standing for me.

if having a big heart
is your greatest flaw,
he went on,
then i think you're
doing just fine.

us.

we have to leave it all to fate. only it has the
power to determine our lives- the power to
bring us together again. but even so, i hope you
keep me safe in your heart, you consume mine.
because maybe when the time is right, we will
find our way back to one another. and maybe
this time, we won't get it wrong.

they called him
dangerous.

he was my safe.

i'm not the
person i
used to be,
and i could say
the same for you.
maybe this is why
we weren't
meant to work.
we just needed
to help each
other grow,
so one day,
another can
love us as we
truly deserve.

let's confess our love
over coffee-spilled
conversations.

i could fall
apart in you a
thousand times
and still not break.

please stop with the excuses,
the stories,
the alibis.
quit sweetening me with these lies.
slap me with the truth.
shove it in my face.
push it down my throat.

i'm so tired of playing this game.
how many times do i have to pass go to make
this stop?

how many times do i have to leave to make you
keep your distance?

i'm not sure what you
want from me anymore.
you say you love me,
yet never take the time to prove your words.
you're always away for too long,
and i'm not sure where you've gone.

i'm not someone you come
running back to when convenient.
i am not a stopover,
an escape.
i am not your break from reality.

i am the type of person whom
you should need to stay for.
i am the type of person whom
you should want to love.

us.

we hiked to the top of the mountain;
the world shrunk around us.
people appeared as dots.
we sat for hours on the verge of the cliff.
i've always been afraid of heights.
but for the first time in forever,
with you sitting right next to me,
i wasn't afraid of falling.

his lighthouse eyes
always had a way of
bringing me home.

i'm not sure why
i keep running back to you.
it's like i'm on autopilot,
and you're all my
subconscious knows.
before i can stop,
i find myself back in those arms,
hoping maybe this time
they'll protect me.
they never do.
we both know
they never will.
i just wish my brain
would stop battling with
my heart and redirect me
to a safer space.
hoping that,
together,
they would take me
to a place where
I could lie down
and not have to worry
if i would fall,
or if someone
would catch me.

- *broken arms*

you undress me simply
with your being.
you look so good on me.

i never want to
wear anyone else.

since you left,
alone has never
felt so lonely.

you are the perfect balance
of everything i've ever needed
and everything i've ever wanted.

i sat there for hours on end,
watching those lights,
waiting for them to change.
waiting for you to change your mind,
my foot hovered over the pedal,
anticipating a signal or a sign.
anything.
all you ever gave me
were red and yellow lights,
hues of confusion,
tribulation.

and after all of this,
how did you not know
my favorite color is green?

- *i'm tired of waiting for green lights*

it wasn't just his eyes;
it was the way they
looked at me.

how can one person
own so much life?

i'll never forget the
afternoon we spent in bed.
the light shined on your face,
as if the day had risen
just for you.
i wanted to kiss you.
but i didn't dare.
because i knew,
i'd never be able to
embrace you as
gently as the sun.

and in this moment,
i knew she loved you.
and i'm pretty sure,
i did too.

only a strong man
can handle the love
of a powerful woman.

i must admit,
this was all in an effort
to get you back.

- *us.*

stay,
his lips begged.

go,
his actions screamed.

perhaps i've gone
a bit mad,
while you've gone
a bit sane.

now you're
standing right
next to me,
yet more distance
has never stood
between us.

us.

i didn't lose him.
he didn't leave.

i set him free.

i gave him my wings
and fell in love as
he flew away.

you belittle women
to enlarge your manhood.

my inbox remains empty,
just like your promises.

- modern love

you were heaven and hell
and all the earth in between.
you were the ecstasy
of my addiction,
constantly keeping me
coming back for more.
you were everything right,
and all things wrong.

you ruined me-
better yet,
destroyed me.
you brought out
the monster i never
knew lived inside.

i can't even fathom how
every time i look
in a mirror,
all I see is you.

but get this,
i would do it all again
without any hesitations.
because,
you see,
we almost made it.
we *almost* made it.
i'd go through
it all for a chance
to see you again.

us.

friends don't love like this.

- friends with benefits

like a masquerade,
we hid behind masks
and danced the night away,
pretending to be
everything we always
wished we could be.
together,
we moved to the
rhythm of the music,
tripping over each other's feet.
we were awful dancers
and even worse lovers.
because once the
music stopped,
i actually took my mask off.
this whole time,
i thought you had removed
your disguise.
but you cowardly hid behind
your façade.

oh what a fool i was
to believe your front,
when i should have been
watching my back.

- masquerade ball

i want to steal
those fingers
and make them
my own.

- *your touch*

i cannot
exist only
having
half
of
you.

us.

he came to me with
pins and needles in
his heart and a limp in his step.
he came to me with
a brokenness i'd never
tasted before,
an edge too jaded to touch.
he came to me
sprinkled in drugs,
begging i'd be his rehab.
he dropped to his knees,
asking for healing,
pleading for fixing.

when all was done,
and he was cured,
i'm pretty sure it was
him who had saved me.

i'll never regret you.

i just wish i could forget.

he was lost.
you could see it in his eyes:
the way they wandered
with no clear direction.

it was beautiful how
he searched for himself
in other people,
as if he was looking for
a person to call home.

i've checked myself
into rehab.
you're my drug of choice,
and honestly,
it's gotten a bit out of hand.
you live in my mind.
they ask me where it hurts,
everywhere.

they ask me where it hurts,
nowhere.

- you've made me go numb

us.

and if i had known
those hands would
leave me in ruins,
i never would have
reached out for them
in the first place.

they keep saying
it's all going to
make sense one day.
i don't know.
time only seems to
add to the madness.
but maybe one day,
i'll wake up next to
you smiling,
because they
were right.

us.

he talks so much,
yet says nothing
at the same time.

if I would tell you how I really feel,
we could figure this whole thing out.
but every time I try confessing,
nothing ever comes forward.
for someone who has a way with words,
you sure know how to put me
at a loss for them.

i'm not sure
why i'm so scared
of loving you.

oh baby,
see here's where
you've gotten it all wrong.
i never needed you.
i wanted you.

there is a difference.

us.

you are my sea.

you are my shore.

- ocean talk

i can never
sleep at night.
i'm haunted
by you.
all of you.
those fingers,
those eyes,
those lips,
those legs,
your body.

oh,
that's just putting
you vaguely.

if i had to choose
between him or the road,
somehow the road seems
less lonely.

these legs were not yours
for the opening.

i used to love the way
he ran back to me,
as if i was his home.
but i no longer have
the energy to house
the ones who only live
to break me.

i can watch you come
and go a hundred times,
all with the hopes that
possibly today,
my love will be enough
to make you stay.

you look so lyrical.

i want to make
poetry out of you.

like rain on a window,
i can see you,
but not feel you;
hear you,
but not touch you;
admire you,
but not love you.

you sit behind glass,
teasing me,
showing me how
stunning a storm can be,
yet not allowing me
 to dance in its wake.

i live to watch you pour,
flood the streets,
drench the
neighborhoods.

you are so beautiful.
i want to be struck
by your devastation.

i can feel myself
falling into your quicksand.

i must get out
before it's too late.

running back
to each other.

it's what we do.
it's all we know.

she's not me,
but i think you
already knew this.
even so,
you continue to turn to her,
searching for something
within the depths of her soul.
i'm not there.
it's ruining you
and destroying her.
it's overtaking
the two of you.
when she's had enough
of loving a man
who doesn't even see her,
she will look into
those eyes and see
my memory replaying.

how is it fair to expect her
to stay with a man
who is clearly in love
with someone else?

i took you off.

i've never felt
so warm.

us.

and if you've
forgotten,
our love will
forever be
weaved within
the fibers of
these pages.

if you confess
your sins to me,
i'll confess
my love for you.

- you don't scare me

us.

you played my body
like an orchestra,
pulling strings,
hitting keys,
notes,
octaves.

the bedroom our arena,
the floor our stage.

and now you've got me
screaming,
begging
for an encore.

my love
would've
completely
destroyed you
anyways.

us.

when i tell the
story of you,
petals fall from
my mouth.
then i find myself
walking in the
garden of you,
strolling through
the endless fields
of potential,
lost in the infinite
crops of what-ifs.

the best thing i ever
did for me
was walking away
from you.

that's the thing about boys:

they always come back.

i've evicted you
from my heart,
but now you
live in the
darkest corners
of my brain.
you are not
welcome here.
this body is no
longer your family.

- permanent tenant

i'm still trying
to understand
how someone
who took
commands
from the devil
could also look
so much like
poetry.

he called it
true love.

i called his
bluff.

- i fold

they won't all
hurt me like you.

- i've got to keep reminding myself

and what would
i be saying to myself
if i took you back
after all of this?

still to this day,
you are my
favorite goodbye.

- i'm trying to find the good in goodbye

maybe,
when we're ready,
we'll meet again.

i can't seem to
remember the good
without the company
of the bad.

this is how i know
i've moved on
from you.

we began as strangers
and ended in
the same manner.

- i'm not even sure who you are anymore

oh,
thank goodness
they weren't you.

- to my future lover

i'm putting down this pen,
closing the book of you.
these words won't
bring you back.
this book won't
make you stay.

my love can't even
remember your face.
this heart of mine doesn't
have a place for you anymore.

us.

you.

this,
my darling has
all been for you.

because without you,
all of this would
be for nothing.

without your soft skin,
i'd never know kind.
without your hands,
i'd never know strength.
without your eyes,
i'd never know beauty.
without your soul,
i'd never know love.

without you,
i would be nothing.

and what an
awful place to live:
a world without you.

as humans,
our wants always
seem to surpass our needs.
we always want what we can't have,
using the irony as an excuse,
as if we have no control
over our decisions.

but we do.

maybe if we spent
a little more time
chasing the things we need,
then maybe we wouldn't
feel so unsatisfied with
the things we want.

us.

can't you see?

the clouds paint
the sky,
leaves change
colors,
and the flowers
bloom for you.

the ocean stands,
and the sun
falls to its knees,
all just for you.

the universe is
obsessed with you.

how could it not be?

the power of a
woman should
never lay
between the
arch of her legs.
the power of a
woman should
live in her brain;
it should come from
her intelligence,
from inside her.
it should come
pouring out of
all the things
she's ever adored,
all the things she's
ever loved.

a woman should
never be praised
for her eroticism.
she should be
celebrated for
her humanity.

never let the fire
that lives in your
soul burn out.

stop dulling yourself
down for people
who cannot handle
your edge.

us.

you must:
fall before you fly.
burn before
you come alive.
completely shatter
before you rebuild.

girls like us weren't
meant to be tamed.
we were born to
run wild and naïve,
made to be recklessly free.

we were put on earth
to shake up this world,
create earthquakes
with our love.
we were not meant
to be forgotten.
we were created
to be eternally exquisite.
we were destined
for beauty.

spend some time with yourself. take yourself on dates. buy yourself coffee and flowers. take yourself on a road trip, blaring your favorite music the entire way. sing in the shower, and dance naked in your bedroom. cook dinner alone. eat alone. sleep alone. learn to truly love yourself. you will find yourself growing in directions you never dreamed possible. your dreams and aspiration will become accomplishments; the world will be placed beautifully at your feet. see, the thing about life is, we must learn to love ourselves before we can even think about loving another. we must be comfortable in our own skin before we crawl into someone else's.

know it's okay
if today all you did
was hold yourself
together.

- i'm proud of you

us.

the destruction
is not the end,
but a new beginning.

do not give up on love- no matter your age or your circumstance, no matter who left or who hurt you. forget all the mistakes and regret. forget all the disappointment and heartbreak. forget. forgive. never stop believing in the magic of love. stop settling for love inferior to your worth, for anything but butterflies fluttering on a warm spring morning, breakfast in bed on a Sunday, slow dancing in the rain. you deserve spontaneous kisses, undeniable passion, real love. never settle and give up on love. never give up on your heart. it's the one thing keeping you alive.

if love is
not a game,

then why are
we still keeping score?

it's a shame
how we starve
our bodies
for the sake
and approval
of others.

- you are perfect the way you are

i hope you never
let the music produced
within you die out.
blare your song.
blast the speakers.
let the harmony dance out
from your eyes
and leave a little beat
every place it falls.
we weren't meant to
live this life in silence.
play on my friend,
and never stop
composing.

your body is your home.
it is a space completely
 of your own.
decorate it how you please.
dress it how you want.
paint the walls,
cover them with art,
tattoo them with beauty.

but please,
you must never let
anyone take your
home away from you.
lock the doors to keep
out the intruders.
leave no welcome mat
at your front door.
never allow anyone to barge in.

it is so important
to keep your home your own.
because once the uninvited get in,
you'll never feel safe again.

no amount of makeup
will cover what
lays beneath.

- *inner beauty*

here,
see what i've done?
i've poured my
heart and soul out,
just for you.

i've emptied myself
in the hopes of refilling
your vacant spaces.
i'm draining myself
to pour my essence
into you.

see,
my love,
i'd slave over these pages,
dying for the words
to help save you.

- and i hope it helps

us.

never allow
loneliness
to lead you
into the
wrong arms.

you need to spend
less time flirting
with the past
and more time
toying with
the present.

promise me you will never give up on yourself
or your dream. you will never settle for love
that doesn't rob you of your sleep. promise me
you will dance until your feet give out, and you
will laugh until waterfalls pour from your eyes.
promise me you will never stop growing, never
stop searching. evolving. promise me you will
put your needs first. above all, promise me you
will always choose to love yourself first.

why do we mourn
the loss of an individual
who willingly left?

we should be celebrating
their freeing departure.

one day,
we'll look back
and laugh at how insecure
and worried we were about life.
we'll realize how
all the things we thought
were breaking us were only
helping lead us to a healed place.
on this day,
we will realize the
irony of life and will
understand how it
all does work out in the end.
and we will be sitting there,
blissfully thankful
for all the confusion and pain.

the end is beautiful.

i can't wait to see you there.

we have food on the table,
a roof over our heads,
love in our hearts.

- we are blessed beyond belief

us.

love never
wanted to be so cruel.
love never
wanted to cause so much pain.

love never
asked for any of this.

- we just made him this way

wealth has nothing
to do with money
and everything
to do with one's
character.

sadly,
sometimes it's too late.

and that's the thing about time,
we cannot get it back.

it's the ones we
cannot write about.

these are the best
types of people.

us.

everything fades:

looks,
scars,
memories,

the pain.

maybe we should
start focusing
on saving ourselves
instead of saving
one another.

they keep telling me
it's the little things
in life that are important,
but i think they're wrong.
it's the big things-
the moments we
realize we'll never
be the same,
the moments that
rob our precious breath.
it's the exact moment
when all our hopes
and dreams come true.
those are the instances
worth dying for.
they are what this
life is all about.

- it's the big things in life

if we don't enjoy the pain,
then why do we
carry it around
with so much pride?

the color of your skin
does not bother me.
the size of your house
does not concern me.
the faith of your religion
does not faze me.
the number in your
bank account
does not impress me.
the identification
of your gender
does not matter to me.

it's the volume of
your heart
and the capacity of
your love
which astonishes me.

our bodies are
vessels for our souls,
not dumping grounds
for our insecurities.

i would willingly
destroy myself
every night
to watch you rise
every morning.

- an ode to the reader

it seems you need
a little less them,
and a little more you.

it's up to us
to find beauty
in the things
meant to break us.

- beauty is everywhere

they did not break you;
you broke yourself.

they did not pain you;
you hurt yourself.

they cannot rebuild you;
you must fix yourself.

they cannot always love you;
you must love yourself.

look at your heart.

after everything
it's been through,
it still hasn't
missed a beat.

it's time to move on.

- overdue

it is such a pity how
we waste our words,
waste our moments.

we only get one shot to get
this whole life thing right.
and we discard so much of it.

if there's something
you've been wanting
to say or something
you've been wanting to do,
if there's something
killing you,
or something keeping
you alive,
find the strength.

i hope you have
the strength to do whatever
it is you want to do,
to live this life how you
were meant to.
and if not,
i hope you find it soon.

it is up to you to find
the power,
the being,
the love in you.

no one else is going
to do it for you,
because no one else can.

love will destroy you
in the most beautiful way.

- you must let it

girls like us should
come with a caution sign.

- warning, danger

while you are out
searching for some place
to make a home,
don't forget to
look within yourself.

it will
always be there.

i promise.

we do not all
think the same,
feel,
hurt,
or heal the same.

we do not all
love the same.

- we are all individuals here

i hope you
find happiness
and love soon.
you deserve to.

- *we all do*

seasons change.
winter and summer
exchange greetings.
days turn to months,
then suddenly,
years have somehow
passed by us.
the world keeps moving.
and all we can do is
evolve with the tides
and howl at the moon.

us.

what a shame
to live in the
confinement
of others'
opinions.

if you drained so much
of yourself into the
wrong hands,
imagine how you'll ravish
in the right arms.

- never give up on love

your scars are the most
beautiful thing about you.

it is beautiful
to be soft,
but it is difficult.
extremely hard.
bad things will
always exist;
there is no
denying it.
but even
with their existence,
good will always
come back around.

open your heart;
set its doors on fire.

be soft.
be beautiful.

us.

what an
underrated
privilege
to wake up
next to
the same man
each morning.

who knows
what will happen tomorrow,
let alone a year from now?

life's unpredictability
is stunning.

enjoy today,
the here and now.

enjoy your life,
one day at a time.

perhaps
we're not too much,
they're just too little.

anger is toxic and will lead you nowhere. it will
only cheat you from your happiness. your
kindness. your sweetness. open the bottle and
release of all the anger you have collected. free
your heart from the rage. the fury. let go of the
resentment. bitter does not look good on you.
anger does not suit you.

us.

silence
heals nothing.
words
will save us all.

we are taught
at a young age to hide
behind our emotions.
soft is weak.

no.
soft is beautiful.

you are under
no obligation
to spend time
with people
who make you
feel lonely.

there's no
reason
to look
back.
the past
hasn't
changed.
it's still
the same.

us.

the next time you
start thinking
you are invincible,
remember how
you are made.
you are stitched
together from brittle bones
and delicate flesh.
you've got a mind
made of magic
and a stained glass heart.
you are not indestructible.

you will break.

but oh,
you will also heal.

less hurt.
more love.

- what we all need

the weakest
of people
are those who
block out love
in fear of
getting hurt.

- *i've been there too*

the next time you
find yourself
drowning in
your insecurities,
remember the
vastness of the ocean.

you are not anchored
down to one spot.
swim away.

set yourself free.

we see the
world through
filters and edits.

open your eyes,
not everything
is as it appears.

maybe we,
ourselves,
are "the one"
we've been
searching
for all along.

some people
are better left
in the past.

- you must leave them there

life is not complicated;
we have just
constructed
it this way.
nothing is for certain
or is perfect.
life is a reflection
of what you make of it.

and when you
get the chance,
i hope you create
something beautiful.

us.

the happiness we create
with our own bare hands
is better deserved
than the joy fed to us
from another's palm.

you have
hurricanes
inside of you.
storms turn
at your
command.

yes,
it is simple
not to feel.
it is easier to
block out the pain,
to cover it up,
drown it out,
throw it away.
they say time heals all,
and you're still
hoping for their
words to be true.
sometime between
hurting and waiting
you've decided
to turn yourself off.

numb is not a feeling;
it is frail.

do not be afraid to feel,
because the pain will
go as easily as
joy will come.

how beautiful
to walk away
from something
not meant for you
with poise.

come,
lie down next to me.
let me take those bags
from under your eyes.

here,
let me love you
like no one has
dared before.

thank the ones who left, the ones who never came back, the ones who freed you from their undeserving grasp. thank the ones who tried to destroy you, but failed. thank the ones who were unkind. thank the ones who only fed you lies. it's time to say thank you to the ones who never treated you as you deserved. the ones who weren't even worth your time, it is them who you need to thank. they are the ones who taught you more than anyone else. they are the ones who made you stronger. braver. kinder. they are the ones who helped create you. thank them from the cracked curves of your heart and the jagged edges of your soul. thank the people who hurt you the most. thank them deeply. thank them gently. thank them boldly. thank them repeatedly.

never stop thanking them.

- thank you, truly

our persistent
need for the
things not
meant for us
will lead to our
demise.

forgive the world,
for he didn't mean
to be so unkind to you.

us.

we should
live to raise
each other up,
not die to pull
each other down.

some people
never change.

it is unfair
to expect
them to.

you've spent so much
of your life doing
what others expect of you.

i think it's time
you start doing things
for yourself.

my sweet friend,
i hope you find happiness soon. i hope you find the place that feels like home and a heart whose beat sounds like family. i hope you travel to all the places you've ever wanted to and see all the things that fill your throat with appreciation. i hope the light kisses your skin and the ocean messes up your hair. i hope you find your passion, and when it calls, i hope you answer. i hope you never give up on the things you want out of life, or yourself. i hope you find someone who sees the light dancing within your soul and never tries to put you out. i hope they bring you flowers and make you tea. i hope they tell you all the things your ears have been burning to hear. i hope you feel special every day and wake each morning with gratitude in your bones. i hope you find all the things you have been searching. i hope you are full of memories and stories. i hope you find your spot in this world, and when you do, i hope you fill it with elegance and love.

us.

grieve.
understand.
accept.
move on.
let it go.

- this is how you heal

if there is anything
i want you to remember,
it would be to
fall in love with yourself.

love yourself.
nothing else matters.

be proud of everything you have gone through, but mostly, what you've become. stop being so hard on yourself. everything will make sense to you one day. all the pain, hurt, and frustration will become worth it.

you are perfect in every way, especially with your flaws. acknowledge the things making you different while embracing everything making you unique. even though you think you are broken, there is so much beauty in your pain. also, you're really not as broken as you think you are. you are stronger than anything that has tried to tear you down. you are a survivor, not a victim. so try not to be so hard on yourself.

create a meaningful life for yourself, one you can be proud of. promise me you will make the most of it all. never let anyone get in the way of your goals in life. more importantly, never give up on your passions and your dreams. do not waste your time on people who do not believe in you. only surround yourself with people who encourage and inspire you.

so breathe, be patient, and trust the course of your life. let go of all the expectations you have created in your head. accept reality as it comes. accept life for what it is.

try not to rely too much on others for your happiness. at the end of the day, all you are guaranteed is yourself, never forget this. stop worrying so much about relationships.

be patient and stay positive while waiting for love. just because you have not found it yet, does not mean you don't deserve to be loved. you must learn to completely love yourself before you even try to love another.

love without the fear of pain. and if you do not find the strength to do so, just make sure you find enough love for yourself.

you are so strong my dear. you have been through a lot and come out on the winning end. the world has tried to break you, but you never let it. thank your past, for it has made you into a better person today. not everyone you have met is meant to stay around forever.

us.

in this book i've
written out my soul,
just for you.

i've written these poems,
these words,
just for you.

i wrote this to remind
you of how truly
astonishing you are,
how earth-shattering,
mountain-moving,
sun-burning,
beautiful you are.

i wrote this to tell you the
things you seem to have forgotten,
the things this world
has told to you differently.
the things you
have told to yourself differently.

sweet girl,
you deserve so
much more than these words.

i am hopeful,
soon enough,
you will find what you've
always been searching for.

and when you do,
i hope it's everything
you've ever imagined.

us.

us.: a collection of poetry
is a book
about healing
and heartbreak.
it tells the journey
of self-love
and the power it holds.
love is everywhere,
but you must let go
of the pain to feel its magic.
thank you for reading.
without you,
the reader,
i'd be nothing.

- about the journey

Made in the USA
San Bernardino, CA
20 January 2018